Before They Leave Here, While They Are With Us

Written by: Dr. Mervin A. Jenkins

Copyright © 2023 by Dr. Mervin A. Jenkins.

All rights reserved.

Dedication

"And let us consider how we may spur one another on toward love and good deeds, not giving up meeting together, as some are in the habit of doing, but encouraging one another."

— Hebrews 10:24-25

Giving thanks to the Most High, without whom there would be no miracles nor mercy. This book is dedicated to family and a gift from us to you. Although we are each responsible for our actions, no one among us can traverse this journey in life alone.

Mother "TIME," Mary. Over "TIME," you have woven your dreams and poetry into the tapestry of each of our lives.

Grandma Ellis (affectionately called Mamie Lee), you are the "LISTENER." You are the living embodiment of what remains of the fondest childhood memories provided by you, your mother (and our "MATRIARCH") Mary Lee (Dollie) Gilliard, and so many other strong community figures.

Aunt Betty, the "CHRONICLER." You blazed the trail and left a path for so many of my siblings and cousins to follow. You have always wanted to see the very best in us all, and you have managed to capture so many of these moments. Keep collecting the memories.

Chiffon (my wife), may you always remember that I am forever thankful that the Most High saw fit for us to share a life together. You are such a beautiful and intelligent person. I remain honored to serve as your lifelong partner. Love to our children, Tauren and Mariah; it is a blessing to see them grow into the people they have both become. To my siblings, I love you each unconditionally:

Dexter, the "FIGHTER." You are indeed champion, both in and outside of the ring!

Melissa, the "TRAVELER." We see the world through your exploits! Never stop immersing yourself in the different cultures and among the people who create them.

Malcolm, the "SEEKER." You hold the wisdom of all who have come before you. Use it to grow stronger as you navigate the path ahead.

Melvin, our "INSPIRATION." You are the first superhero I ever knew. Thank you for allowing each of us to watch you set our course in life, leading by example. Job well done!

"Dreamers and Doers"

by Mervin A. Jenkins

She knew the floor plans.

And with his gifted hands at her command,

they unite, the dreamer and doer.

From a school of hard knocks

to a life built with blocks,

they unite, the dreamer and doer.

For what is a dream once asked?

To which I answer alas,

incomplete without a doer.

And yet we've seen

doers without dreams,

lost and without future.

Do not be fooled

nor ever should we pretend,

We need not both dreamer and doer.

Written: 2014

Inspired by my mother, Mary E. Jenkins, my first teacher/poet,

and my father, Melvin Jenkins, my first superhero.

Table of Contents

Chapter One: Time Is Not on Your Side 1

Chapter Two: Why Aren't You There Yet?................................8

Chapter Three: What Is a Picture Worth? 14

Chapter Four: Listen to Them..19

Chapter Five: I Ain't Mad at Cha...24

Chapter Six: Before They Leave Here 29

Chapter Seven: Before You Leave Here..................................32

Chapter Eight: In Conclusion, We Have Now! 35

Chapter One: Time Is Not on Your Side

It's a cool winter day 2022. It's actually the day after Thanksgiving, and my wife and I sit with my dad as he tells us his thoughts on losing a parent. He should know, he's lost both of his. I would even go so far as to say that he is an expert on the subject. For most of my life, I have told myself it will be extremely difficult to face life and move forward when my parents are no longer living. Before you tell 50-year-old me, "Hey, it could be you before them," keep in mind I'm referring to the scenario that plays out if life were to go about its natural course. That natural course, often referred to as the great circle of life, is simply a natural pathway for the living that usually consists of the oldest of us dying prior to those who are younger, with the process repeating as it passes from one generation to the next. For many, the emotional toll of thinking about this can be both physically and mentally draining. For others though, they find peace in the process and embrace it, while being more accepting of our last living experience before our great transition. These very emotions and my overall thoughts on the subject have made me even more conscious and attuned to how I interact with my loved ones. This is especially true of the elderly, who have sacrificed so much to put many of us in positions to capitalize on opportunities they were not as fortunate to have presented to them during the prime of their lives.

When I got my very first leadership position, it can only be described as a surreal moment in my life. I call these "sword in the stone" moments, and they usually signal a chain of events that set us up for life moving forward and all that it entails. If you are familiar with the story of King Arthur and his pulling the sword from the stone, you already know there was a story arc built around a young person trying to traverse a labyrinth of obstacles while growing into adulthood. Oftentimes, this labyrinth-of-life we are placed in makes it difficult to fully realize how our responses to various obstacles will impact our life's journey. For example, I found advancing into my first role as a school administrator a "sword in the stone" moment because for the first time, I was able to see myself doing something I thought I would never be able to do: lead others. It was one of the many "sword in the stone" moments in leadership that I would go on to experience. Thanks to my mother, other family members, and some awesome college professors, I eventually obtained a job as a school leader at a prominent school and district in the state of

North Carolina. One of the very first things I did after securing this job that I speak of was going to visit my mom, at my parents' home, which was just over a three-hour drive away in South Carolina at that time. I did this to personally thank my mother for her constant encouragement over the years. I could not imagine, at the time, just how far my newly found position, passion, and purpose in society would actually take me.

As with many parents, especially mothers, they are often our first protectors and champions. They teach us that we can achieve even what we may find seemingly impossible at various junctures in our life. I witnessed firsthand how my mom did her very best to halt any thought of self-doubt that would come upon me, regardless how big or small the challenge. She still does it to this day, too. When I made that trip home to South Carolina from North Carolina, years ago, it was an unannounced visit. I called from my cell phone to make sure my mom was around, but I did not tell her I was coming home to see her in person. I cherish the memory of having done this because I was fortunate enough, then and now, to still have my mother here living to hear me say, "Thank you..." When I stepped out of the car, she was actually sitting on her patio, right outside the front door of their home in Eutawville, South Carolina. If my memory serves me correctly, I actually said, "Thank you for saving my life, Mom." You see, by this time, I had lived long enough to witness many family, friends, and associates make poor life choices that had resulted in either their untimely death, incarceration, or very unfortunate living circumstances. It has been well over 20 years now since I held this conversation with my mom. Looking back, it was my attempt at giving her the flowers she deserved while she was still living. This is obviously not the case for everyone, but for those whose family members are still here and you have yet to give them their flowers, at a time when they can still smell them, you should.

Here's something to think about: I remember our school family losing one of our custodial staff members to a sudden heart attack some years ago. It was obviously unexpected and took many of the staff by surprise. Less than a week after this, I attended the funeral services for that employee. My supervisor at the time walked up to me at the funeral and softly gave his condolences about the loss to our school family. Immediately afterwards, he asked me, "How are the interviews going to fill the position?" I was totally caught off guard by the question, considering the place and time, and I still honestly can't say how or even if I responded—although I'm sure I did. What I do remember is walking away and thinking how true it was that life does indeed go on without us—sometimes without compassion.

Fact is, as of today, there is still a generation of elderly who predate modern day technology. For example, my grandmother on my mom's side of the family is 90 years old. She, like many in her demographic, will likely never sit down at a computer and use it as a means of gathering information or creating something. Yes, there are the exceptions to this statement, but I speak of the majority who make up this subgroup, or "silent" generation, as they are sometimes referred to as. My current position in life requires that I work from day to day. Some days are busier than others, but amidst the numerous Zoom calls and trainings, I have small pockets of time. We can easily coax ourselves into believing we don't, but that only becomes a reality if we let the rigor of our day-to-day consume us. Therefore, I must take it upon myself to decide how much interaction I will have with my grandmother who still lives in my hometown an hour-and-a-half away. This also applies to my mother, my father, and a plethora of relatives who still live in the town I grew up in. Phone calls are the easiest method for staying connected to them. Fortunately, in my grandmother's case, her hearing remains sharp, so we can both enjoy a conversation without strain whenever we do speak. One of my greatest moments with my grandmother and mother was having them both, along with my wife and other family and friends, witness me deliver a keynote at Benedict College—my alma mater in Columbia, South Carolina. This was not the first time I had delivered a keynote, nor would it be the last. However, it would have been easy to not go through the preparations it took to get everyone there and simply say, "I'll do it next time." We know that nothing is promised to us, especially time. Keep that in mind whenever you think about doing something with a loved one and procrastinate because you believe that time will be on your side—it's NOT!

Mommy Mary, Mother Time... My mother has always recognized the effects that time has on everything. She says that some people value their time more than money. "Once that time is gone, it's gone—you can't put a price on it." "If you could turn back time, what would you do differently?" I asked my mother once. "I'm not quite sure," she responded.

Many times, we look back and say what we would have done differently, but in reality, we are likely to repeat the same thing all over again. She does agree, however, that there are many things she could have done differently. Her example was graduating high school and having gone straight to a 4-year college versus technical school and then directly into the workforce. However, this is all relevant to the times we live in. Today, there's a huge argument that the technical school pathway versus the 4-year college is probably more suitable for preparing you for career opportunities.

Chapter Two: Why Aren't You There Yet?

Our parents took us everywhere! This also applies to anyone who took the parenting role in helping you become the person you are today. Okay, yes, it was probably more of a duty than just their sheer willingness and desire to transport you to some place fun, exciting, and exotic. Obviously the trips to Disney World, Universal Studios, Six Flags, or Carowinds were for you, but the romantic trips to Hilton Head or the Poconos damn sure weren't. Still, they managed to make the best of memories with their little bundle—or bundles, if you were sharing the backseat with brothers and sisters—of responsibility that they brought into this world to share it with them. If you were raised by a single parent, or grandparents, or other family members, this still applies. After all, it was still likely a team effort. Now that you know I'm not leaving anyone out, regardless of who raised you, let's get back to the subject of this chapter—traveling.

I'm asking you to do something memorable with your loved ones as it relates to seeing the world. This is another one of those "waiting until the time is right" scenarios that I don't want anyone to miss. If I'm being honest, I have yet to do it with my own parents. My dad finds peace of mind at home, which is where he worked as a self-employed auto mechanic. He makes it clear to me and the rest of the family that he has no desire to go beyond the comfort of his home-state of South Carolina. Even within that geographic range, he's prejudiced to the low-country region of the state. However, my mother is an adventurer at heart. While she has traveled a fair amount, she's never left the Americas before, outside of a cruise with friends through the Caribbean many years ago now. Nonetheless, although not an easy feat, there should be more opportunities and moments for travel. Here's where siblings can be a great asset. In my case, I have a younger sister who's a traveling nurse and served two tours in Iraq with the National Guard some years ago. As if her travels for her career weren't enough, she's also vacationed in some of the coolest places on the planet. My point is that she loves to travel. We all, to some degree, live vicariously through her exploits—both personal and professional. She, along with my mom's sister, will soon be accompanying my mom on their vacation to Dubai. While it doesn't take me off the hook from doing something similar with my mother, I do find peace in knowing that the little girl, my mom, who yearned to see the world will be seeing a little more than she perhaps had expected to in her lifetime. Oh, they even have a half-day layover in Paris, France! Personally, I can't wait to hear about their experiences together abroad.

There are so many reasons why we don't get to take a grand trip with the people who raised us and are still living. However, life does seem to always get in the way of making leisure travel, or vacationing, a reality. In fact, there's no way I could possibly address every single one of those challenges. Whatever your reasons may be, they are likely tied to the responsibilities you have in your life right now. Demanding jobs that require an insane amount of work hours to maintain your lifestyle can be one. Maybe it's the fact that you now have a family of your own, and you're barely able to secure the resources to get them out to see the world beyond their front yard, backyard, or bedroom window. All I can say is if your parents were able to do it, there should be no excuse stopping you from doing the same. That said, there's nothing wrong with not doing it if traveling doesn't bring your parents joy. The last thing we want to do is put someone, especially people so instrumental in our lives, in a position that they would prefer not to be in.

I'll end this chapter by reminding us all that there are numerous ways to see the world in this day and time. If a loved one doesn't want to fly, you can certainly get them on a train. If that is not an option, for whatever the reason, there's always a nice cruise ship pulling out from a port in driving distance from you. Even my own dad, the reluctant traveler, was persuaded to take a cruise many years ago. It's one of his fondest memories, and he talks about it often. He still recalls being on what he described as "a city on the sea." He loved the energy that permeated every level of the ship at all hours of the day and into the wee hours of the morning. "The food, so much food," he would say. He loved the noise that spilled from the casino rooms and the live shows that are likely the closest he'll ever come to doing Broadway in his lifetime. I still find it funny how he is quick to say he has no desire to do it again, but I find some sense of calm knowing that he did.

Finally, for those who still haven't found a preferred method of travel, there's the automobile. I'm in the United States, so between North and South America alone, there's still so much to see and choose from. For example, if you're in the United States, do you live close to Canada? If you're in Canada, maybe Alaska is right next door? If you're in Mexico, perhaps you wish to explore further south to Panama? Regardless if it's South America or North America, there's so much to see, and it only takes a tank of gas, or a few tanks of gas and a boat ride, to make it happen. So what are you waiting for? Get out there and show a loved one who raised you something that they thought they would never see in their lifetime. Trust me, everyone will remember it.

Little sister Melissa, the traveler... My sister Melissa talks about being open to the idea that there was so much out there. She talked about going to Atlanta, Georgia, from Eutawville, South Carolina, with her middle school buddy and realized the world was bigger than she could have ever imagined. She thanks the military for bringing this revelation full circle. She served in Operation Iraqi Freedom in the early 2000s stationed in Balad, Iraq. This experience made her more aware of different cultures and varied belief systems, both near and far. She says that she became more personable with different cultures and gives thanks to the military for this opportunity. It was during this time she was able to take her leave and visit places like Paris, France, and Amsterdam, Netherlands. Finally, she serves today as a travel nurse, and it fits perfectly with her beliefs on seeing the bigger world. She originally worked about 7 years in the traditional nursing setting before taking her talents on the road as a travel nurse. Since doing this, she has seen almost every geographical region of the United States. Her philosophy is you want to travel and enjoy where you're at but also do it in a way that is financially beneficial to enjoy it even more.

Chapter Three: What Is a Picture Worth?

So there's no excuse for this not happening...take pictures! By the time this book is on your coffee table, we will likely have an iPhone XV available for purchase. How many of us, if we're lucky, only have an obituary of a loved one to remember them by? I get that we take what we can get, but I'd like to think seeing this person captured in a shared moment with us would be so much more gratifying. Maybe you took the picture of them while they were caught up in the moment and didn't even notice you doing it. Maybe you took that digital watch you own and remotely took a picture with you and that person or group of people together. However you might capture that brief snapshot in time, this is one of the things we can do while they are still with us. It's probably the easiest to achieve on my list of to-dos, but many of us still fail to do it. If I'm being fully transparent, we just split the Thanksgiving holiday with my wife's family as well as my own, and not once did any of us pull out a mobile device to capture the moment—any moment.

Have we reduced ourselves to a group of people who have unconsciously taken for granted the idea that there may not be a next time? Perhaps we are in denial, believing that we will always be here to tell the story of what occurred, who was there, and how we felt. Pictures are truly worth a thousand words, and even more than that, a lifetime of memories. Remember that there was once a time when capturing someone's image was something that only the wealthiest of us could afford. It brought great honor and distinction to see a picture drawn of a loved one resting above the great room's fireplace mantle or in the hallway of a home.

If you find yourself falling short or behind in this arena, do not fret. There is usually a family member who has already begun the work for you. My mom's sister, Aunt Betty, is that person in my family. Aunt Betty has maintained a foggy collection of black and whites from the early Polaroid/Kodak-moment era up to today's digital 48-plus megapixel devices. Whenever she's around, the family knows you better be on your best behavior because chances are, whether you know it or not, you're likely being recorded or having your picture taken—sometimes both. While it can be annoying at times, you must admit that there's nothing like having those special moments captured to visually remind us of the best times we shared.

Whenever I visit Aunt Betty, or when she's around, I can always count on having these wonderful images to reference. Our conversations range from questions about who's who to what were we thinking when this picture was taken. The craziest thing is, even while we find ourselves entangled in those memories, Aunt Betty is capturing new ones by taking more pictures in the present. These memories should rest in the hands of multiple people. Use the technology available to you and have the portfolio shared from your family's "collector of memories," like my Aunt Betty. That way, if one person—for any reason at all—loses this treasure chest of good times among family and friends, someone else will still have them.

Aunt Betty, the chronicler... You've already heard about Betty's affinity for holding fast to the memories made with family and friends. I was sitting with Aunt Betty on her back porch not long ago, and she told me a very emotional story about her time as a nurse in the DMV (D.C., Maryland, Virginia) back in the 1980s. Although she was just a very young and budding professional, she took a liking to a much older woman whom she came to love as she would her own mother. Being so far away from her own family, back in South

Carolina, Betty loved the idea that there was someone around to offer her the guidance and support she could only compare to that of a close family member. Although this lady was not related to Betty, she made sure that whenever Betty was unable to get back home for the holidays and other such occasions, that Betty felt like her place was a home away from home. Anyway, while cleaning out her closet space some time ago, Betty ran across a card from this woman. The card was from almost 40 years ago when she wrote to let Betty know how much she had missed her. By this time, Betty had relocated from the DMV to work as a nurse across the country in California. At the bottom of the card, expressing her longing to know that Betty was doing well in her new setting, the lady had written her phone number. As Betty read the card, now a retired nurse living in Charleston, South Carolina, she reminisced about the love and affection this lady and her family had showered her with all those years ago. Betty decided to call the number to see if there was any chance the number had remained the same. Sure enough, the lady, now in her eighties, answered and was overly joyous knowing that she and Betty were once again in touch with one another. A short time later, both she and Betty were in tears having finally reconnected after all those years.

When I asked my Aunt Betty about her intentionality around taking these pictures, she recalled her mother buying her one of those little Polaroid cameras for Christmas when she was in the neighborhood of about 14 years old or so. Just like that, a small gesture from her mother had transformed Aunt Betty into the keeper of memories.

Chapter Four: Listen to Them

It's important to know that my inspiration for writing this book was my father. While sitting down with my wife and parents at their home during the holidays, I asked my dad about the death of his parents. I wanted to know what he was most proud of and what, if anything, he wished he'd done differently. My dad is a simple man who has never wanted more in life than to afford a comfortable living and be positioned to help family when they needed it most. To this day, he has little tolerance for stupidity but tends to go out of his way when someone is trying to do their best with what little resources they have. I heard him say to me, "Mervin, you listen." I know this makes him proud. The fact that he still serves as a role model and someone I look up to is therapy for the both of us. For him, it's about a sense of pride, and for me, a sense of security. I believe this shared experience can bring the same feelings of warmth to anyone, especially the elderly, when they feel like we are listening.

My dad was recently diagnosed with vascular dementia, and as a result, he tends to tell the same stories whenever I go home to visit. I always let him tell the stories, although I myself can tell them almost verbatim after hearing them repeated regularly over the years. I love the fact that he himself laughs as he tells one of his funnier stories. I even know the exact spot where he will pause to allow himself to laugh as he tells them. My wife and I just smile and look at one another as soon as he begins. It's our little inside joke, but we both express our love for my dad by listening as intently as we did our very first time hearing the story. I don't know where this habit of listening came from, but I have behaved in this manner for as long as I can remember. As long as the elderly would allow me to listen to them, I did.

My step-great-great grandmother passed when I was a young man. She had lived long enough to retell the horrific tales of her parents being in slavery. She was a proud woman who seemed to carry family near and dear to her heart. She was very old and still lived alone. In my earliest memories of her, she was already in her nineties. By this point in her life, she was known for locking up her house as soon as the sun began to set in the evenings. She would often need to have burning wood piled up in her home near the fireplace each day. My younger cousin and I took pride in being able to help her with this task as often as we could. This usually happened at least every other day since she lived alone and directly across the street from her step-granddaughter, my grandmother. Once the wood was all set and readily available for her to access, I would often stay behind and listen as she told stories from her childhood. I always made an attempt to keep the conversation going by asking questions that would cause her mind to activate memories she still had tucked away in her aging and frail body. There was something about having this knowledge at your fingertips that I could not quite put my hands on at that time. Even I myself can barely remember everything she spoke of, but I knew it gave her a sense of calm. I never forgot how it made her feel, and in some ways, how it made me better. Now, as a man myself, my only regret is not having listened just a little more.

Just how important is listening? I've heard it said that it's so important the Creator only gave us one mouth but two ears. Ever since the dawn of man, our ability to tell stories has been essential to our survival. Just as important are the audience of listeners who retained the knowledge being passed down so that future generations might learn and improve upon them. Listening is what drives us as a people. We do it in our personal lives and at work. When we become master listeners, we become better problem-solvers, in my opinion. Our elders have a lot to say, and they've certainly earned a right to. It's our job to listen to them. By doing so, we become better—better together.

Grandma Mamie, the watcher... When I asked her about her love for listening, she responded that she always loved trying to understand what people were talking about. She says that she remembers her own mother being the more talkative one of the two. Now just a few years shy of the age that her mother lived to be, Mamie still manages to practice the art of listening to this day. She will often quote the familiar phrase, "There's a reason why God gave you only one mouth and two ears, it is so you can do more listening and less talking." Thank God she is this way. Grandma Mamie actually was one of the few people to help recall and tell a mostly forgotten and tragic story that was said to have taken place in our hometown many years ago. I actually reference the tale in a book I'm currently working on titled, "Teachable Moments in Leadership: Sword in the Stone Moments."

The importance of verbally passing down stories from one generation to the next has traditionally helped to usher in every era in the history of mankind. There is much to be learned from they that listen—the watchers.

Chapter Five: I Ain't Mad at Cha

The late rapper Tupac Shakur wrote a song titled, "I Ain't Mad at Cha," which described his undying love for a former gang member. His friend and former partner in crime had changed his way of life after having been arrested and serving time in prison. He basically returns home practicing Islam and expresses to his old friend, Tupac, that he no longer desires to participate in the illegal activity they once did together prior to him being incarcerated. I share that summary to say that if Tupac could garner the strength to forgive his homie for turning away from a life of crime, what excuse do we have?

Nothing pains me more than to hear someone say that they don't have a relationship with a loved one. Personally, I'd like to think that the strained relationships I have in my own life are not for a lack of trying. In this section of the book, it's all I ask of each of us: that we try. When dealing with the elderly, we sometimes come to a point where they may not agree with something we have elected to do or vice versa. This is where agreeing to disagree comes into play. What we should not do is allow our differences to make strangers or, even worse, enemies of us.

Some years ago, I watched as a dear family member lost someone who was probably the most important person in their life. Honestly, from the outside looking in, that person has never been the same since. Quite frankly, it's extremely hard to bring closure to a broken relationship when the other person is no longer here to forgive or be forgiven. It ends up being a "What if...?" moment in our lives. Fact is, almost every single one of us will have a few of those "What if...?" moments in our lifetime. *What if I had played the same lotto numbers I played the day or week before they finally rolled out? What if I had gone to college after high school? What if I had bought the electric car instead of the diesel one?* These are all moments you can still relatively explore to some degree. You can still play those lotto numbers today or tomorrow. You can still apply to college, generally speaking, at any age. However, when you put people into this equation, especially the elderly, that is not always the case. A "What if...?" moment tied to someone who is no longer living is an entirely different beast. At the end of the day, no matter how you spin it, this type of "What if...?" moment will remain seared in our memory for as long as we live.

I have had my fair share of "What if…?" moments over the years. Some years ago, a college buddy who I had known since junior high school tragically passed away. We both lived in the same city when this happened. He had been reaching out to me pretty regularly in the weeks leading up to the accident that took his life. In all honesty, I had been dodging most of his phone calls and requests to hang out because I felt like his lack of responsibility would only compromise the things I had worked hard to achieve. For example, the few times we did get together to hit the town, he would actually hop in my car with an open container of alcohol, which he would try to consume prior to our arriving at our destination. Nonetheless, I reluctantly answered his phone call one Saturday morning, and it turned out he was reaching out to verbally acknowledge the demons and the challenges he was facing. He asked me to help him through it, and I agreed to introduce him to another person who might be able to assist him. The following day, I got a call that my friend had died in a car accident. The guy I was supposed to introduce him to that day was actually sitting and waiting with me for him to arrive when I got the call. All I could do was think: "What if…" I had answered my friend's call earlier and helped to get him the help he needed?

Tell the people you love that you love them. Tell them you love them when they are in full support of what you do and tell them you love them when you disagree. Love is unconditional, and it should therefore transcend any earthly disagreement one might have. Tupac knew his gangsta lifestyle was not conducive to a life of spiritual enlightenment. Still, through it all, he wanted his homie whom he loved to know he held no grudge against him. He wanted him to know that although they could not have the relationship they once had, their unconditional love for one another could never be broken.

Big Brother Dexter, the fighter... I was already in middle school when I found out that my dad had a son with someone else prior to marrying my mom. Although I grew up as the oldest sibling in our household, I now respect him as the big brother to us all. He works for the Orangeburg County Sheriff's Department and has served in law enforcement all of his adult life. He has a passion for boxing that grew into a purpose as he opened a local gym for training young people in the art of boxing. Ironically, Dexter fought his biggest fight during the pandemic. I was present via Zoom when doctors told the family his chances of survival were slim. After over 8 weeks on a ventilator, Dexter came out of an induced coma thinking it was Thanksgiving when it was actually well into the new year. The experience has reminded us all about the fragile framework each of our stories are built upon.

When I asked him about his thoughts on his philosophy surrounding forgiveness, my brother said he almost always looks at the Bible and to the Gospel of Matthew (7:12): "In everything, do to others what you would have them do to you..." He speaks on the principle this is rooted in, saying that it's not about getting back at or even with someone who has wronged you, but rather, finding it in one's heart to treat this person with the respect and dignity you yourself would expect to be given.

Chapter Six: Before They Leave Here

The next two chapters are tied to one another more than any other two chapters in this book. They both involve the writing of a will. This chapter is geared more toward your actual loved one writing their will, while the next chapter focuses on you writing yours.

A will is an important document to assist in the planning of one's estate once they pass. This is obviously a very emotional thing to think about. It's even harder to have this conversation with loved ones who, based on their age alone, may be closer to crossing death's threshold than others in their lives. Having this conversation with someone, like a parent or any other type of guardian, is simply emotionally draining in most instances.

My parents and siblings have touched on the conversation as it relates to my parents and their will. I can tell you the look alone on all of our faces during these hard and heartfelt conversations says it all. Quite frankly, it often leads to the conversation coming to a close even faster than it started. Still, it is important to keep at the forefront the idea that death is not a "maybe" scenario but a *"will* be sooner or later" one—pun intended.

Great-Grandmother, the matriarch... As of the writing of this book, my Great-Grandmother Mary Lee Johnson Gilliard, whom locals affectionately called Daw Daw, is the only one who is deceased. She lived to be 93 years of age and accomplished so much for someone who had spent most of her younger years working the fields of southern landowners and later serving as the "help" in the homes of affluent families in and around the neighborhood back in those days. Daw Daw did not leave a will when she took her last breath in 2012. As close as our family was, there still seemed to be some rather quiet rumbles surrounding who had a right to what in terms of anything of value. She, along with her husband, had taken the time to do other things that made a huge difference in helping to keep things civil between family members. Land that they owned had been signed over to younger family members, and bank accounts had the names of relatives added to carry out future wishes and help to ease any financial burden that may have arisen in their twilight years. For a generation of people born into a society that sought to diminish their contributions in life, I would like to think, job well done.

How many times have you heard stories of families falling apart because their loved ones did not leave behind a will? Perhaps you yourself have had that unfortunate experience? Talk to your loved ones and try to get them to understand that the last thing they want to do is leave behind a messy situation that has made enemies of many siblings and other close family members throughout time. Life is fleeting. Do not put off asking your loved one to go through this process if they haven't already.

Chapter Seven: Before You Leave Here

If you thought the last chapter was hard, this one is slightly harder. Now, we will address preparations for the day you no longer exist in the physical world. Getting your affairs in order is solely about eliminating as much stress as possible for your loved ones who will remain behind.

First, without a will, you leave all of your estate to the authority of the state. While there is some degree of exactly how this is done based on each state's interstate laws, this is basically what it boils down to. If you are a guardian to someone, who will take on these responsibilities? How will your estate be distributed, and to whom? Are you creating a scenario that takes into account your state tax laws? You want to ensure that whoever inherits your estate does not get burned by the tax laws when you are gone. If you plan to gift anything or make a charitable donation, you want to be sure you maximize this contribution and avoid any penalties that may be associated with doing so. Also, remember that you want to create a legally sound document that greatly reduces the chance that loved ones end up fighting the state over what should technically be theirs, or even worse and as mentioned in the last chapter, preventing loved ones from fighting one another.

Finally, not doing a will is another example of a "What if…?" moment you don't get a chance to do again—because you'll be gone. So what are you waiting for? If you have not done this already, please do it—do it now!

Mervin, the creator… Oddly enough, I brought my creative talents to the table when writing my own will. By default, I'm a creator of lyrics, poetry, and art. I began my teaching career as a middle school art instructor, and before that, my love of poetry led me to the hip-hop culture and eventually becoming an emcee. Believe it or not, I took my artistic approach to creating as a starting point to help me begin my own creation of a will to leave behind for loved ones when that day does arrive. Think about it, the visual artist often creates knowing that what they leave behind will have a lasting impact on generations to come. With that in mind, they take careful measures to put forth their best self, knowing it will be something that others will appreciate and cherish as well as be inspired by. Just like one of the scenes in the great Sistine Chapel in Vatican City, I can only hope that my reach to touch others will be well received, remembered, and expanded upon when I am no longer part of this earthly realm we all temporarily call home.

Chapter Eight: In Conclusion, We Have Now!

Daddy Melvin, the inspiration... I began writing this book when my dad was recently diagnosed with vascular dementia. I had seen signs of stress to his memory some years ago, when he began repeating the same stories over again each time I would visit him, sometimes telling the story multiple times in the same sitting. One particular incident led to my mom getting him checked out by a medical professional, and that was good because now we at least have a reason for his sometimes loss of words and repetitive telling of the same story. Even through it all, I try to never say to him anything like, "Dad, you already told me that." Instead, I try to listen as if I have never heard the story before. Why? Well for one, it brings him joy, and I can see it as he smiles and laughs while telling me and other family and friends about his exploits throughout the years. Then there's also the idea that I want to avoid him feeling embarrassed by something that for many is simply a sign of the times.

If there's a remote chance to end this book on a high note, I'll do my best to achieve that right here. The overarching theme throughout this book all ties back to time. The idea of time is probably best described as "Father" to us all who treats us like bastards. Still, just try to remember that we have NOW! By God, if you have to put down this book right this second and call a loved one, STOP and make the call! Go visit them if you're within driving distance. Oh, and I'm an educator by trade, so it's only right if we end this with a homework assignment. I challenge you to reach out to this person or group of people you're thinking of and use the blank page following the prompts below to write about your conversation with them. I'm also including a space for you to take a picture of the moment to place in the book. If you are not able to take a picture in person, do it through a virtual call on a platform like FaceTime or Google Meet. Just be sure to ask their permission. Remember all the things we discussed in the book so far and feel free to talk about any of them. Below, you will find a few potential prompts and questions that are recommended for conversational topics:

1. What does family mean to you? How do you want to be remembered by others? If you could go back, knowing what you know now, what would you have done differently, and why?
2. What has been your greatest accomplishment in life?

3. What was your most memorable vacation?
4. Who inspired you?
5. What were your parents/grandparents like?
6. Who was one of your favorite people to work with, and why? What was the best job you ever had, and why was it such a good job? In your opinion, what should be one's ultimate goal in life?
7. Is there anything you still wish to do in your time left on this Earth?
8. What do you see as the greatest challenge for humanity in the days ahead, and what do you think are solutions for solving this problem?
9. What is one of your favorite movies of all time, and why?
10. How do you think you've made this world a little better than when you came into it?

Now remember, come back here to this book and record the event on the next page. Okay, that's the assignment, see you soon.

Use this space however it works best for you. One suggestion may be placing a picture(s) and writing your notes below. Just immerse yourself in the experience...

Welcome back! So I'm curious, how did it go? Did you talk about traveling somewhere exciting? Maybe you just decided to take a picture? If it was via FaceTime or some video chat feature, hopefully you took a screenshot? Were you able to get your loved one(s) to tell a story? Was it a favorite story that they tell over and over again, or was it something entirely different? Were you able to guide them through the conversation by asking them questions related to the topic? Finally, assuming it was the appropriate person to have that conversation with, *now pun not intended here*, did you discuss their will and yours?

My little brother Malcolm, the seeker... By the time this book is completed, I will have done this activity with him. Malcolm and I have drifted apart, and much of it, in my opinion, revolves around my playing a more father-figure role over the years versus being the big brother. Quite frankly, I realize that the difference in years as it relates to our age has greatly contributed to this divide. This, for me personally, has been one of the things that I wish I could do over again. We both have a love for video games, and I find some of our best conversations relating to new console games and older ones that bring back memories of he and I trying to complete them by beating different level bosses.

I was almost a senior in high school when Malcolm was born, so I will always ask myself: "What if…" Malcolm and I had been born in the same decade or only two or three years apart? Still, there is no time like the present, and the time for change is now!

Regardless of how you respond to these questions, I'm sure the interaction was a heartfelt one that brought a sense of warmth to the conversation. In that alone, my dear friends, lies the beauty of it all. You can repeat this process as many times as you can stand, and it's likely to only build stronger bonds as well as lasting memories. Do what you can because you have now. Do it, before they leave here, WHILE THEY ARE WITH US!

www.LifeThruMusic.com

Made in the USA
Middletown, DE
25 January 2023